A Puppy Poem

By

Katherine B. Parilli

Copyright © 2020

ISBN-13: 978-1-947238-39-8
Kindle Edition 978-1-947238-40-4
Library of Congress Control Number: 2020922165

De Graw Publishing
Okahumpka, Florida

A puppy poem I would love to write,

But what can I say that you do not already know?

Of waggling tails and tender kisses,

Of a heart of love so willing to forgive,

Of gentle acts of unexpected compassion,

And a lifetime of faithful devotion you are already aware.

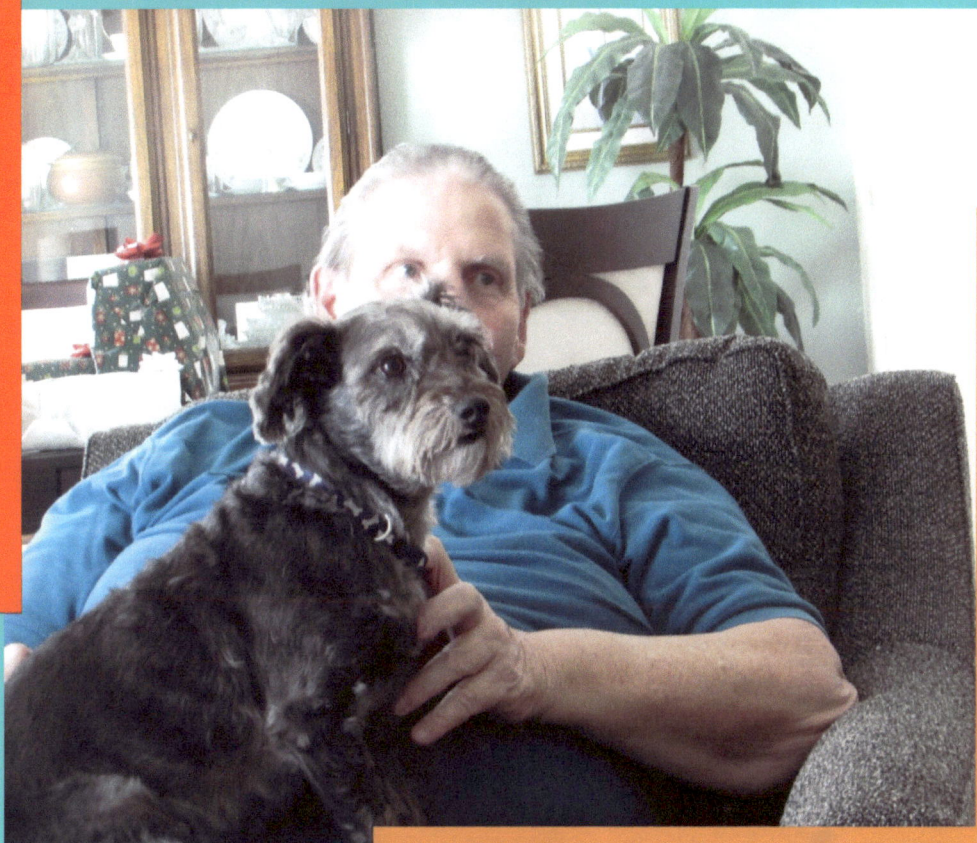

The many acts of selfless
heroism,
And the unbreakable
bonds that flow through
so many stories

Could fill a million
libraries,
And would require a
lifetime to read.

For when the Lord looked down and saw the humble state to which we fell,

His Heart was moved by
our grief.

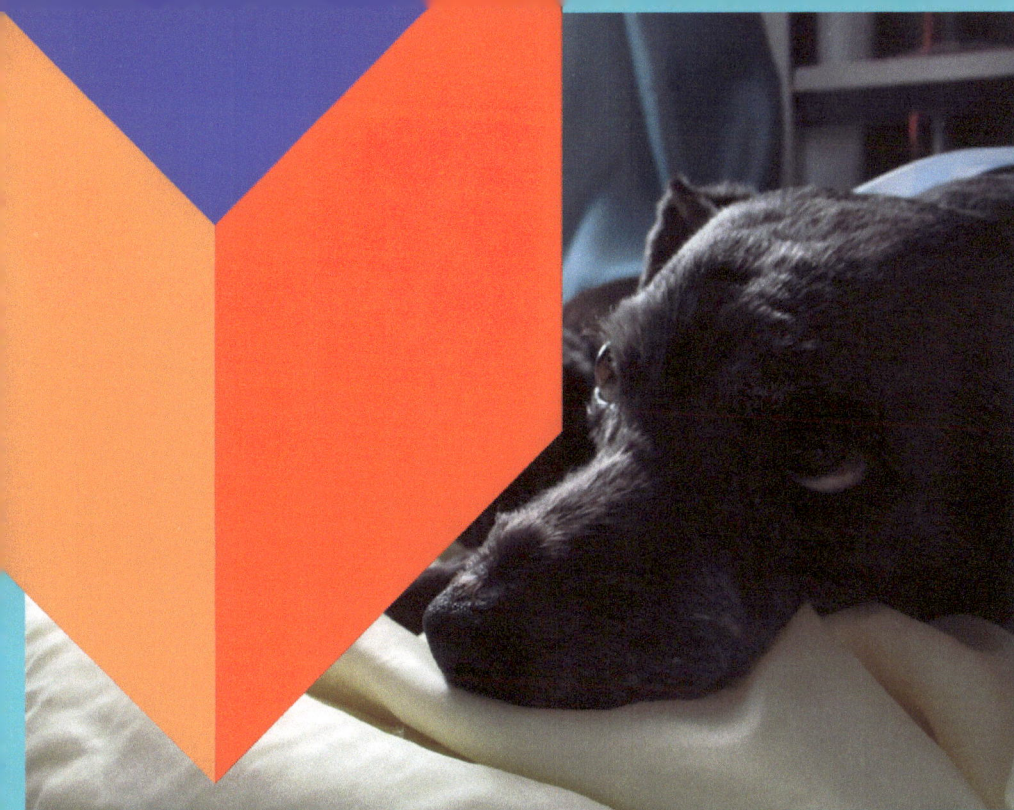

With tears He looked
down and beheld our
lonely trail
and the burdens that
would seek to crush out
our life,

And beheld the fearful
forces that would long to
crush our soul,

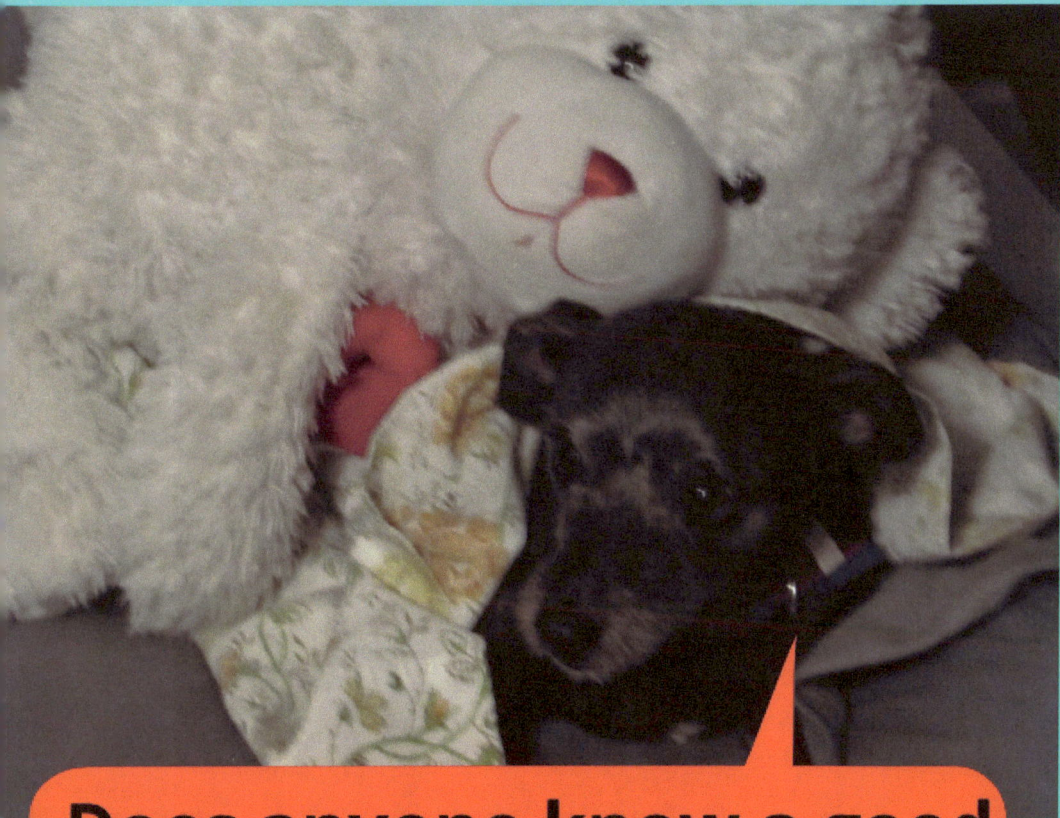

Does anyone know a good place to hide?

And moved by our fearful plight
He sought a way to ease our burdens,

I love you with all
of my heart

And lessen the impact of
our dreadful plight
By sending us a message
of love and hope

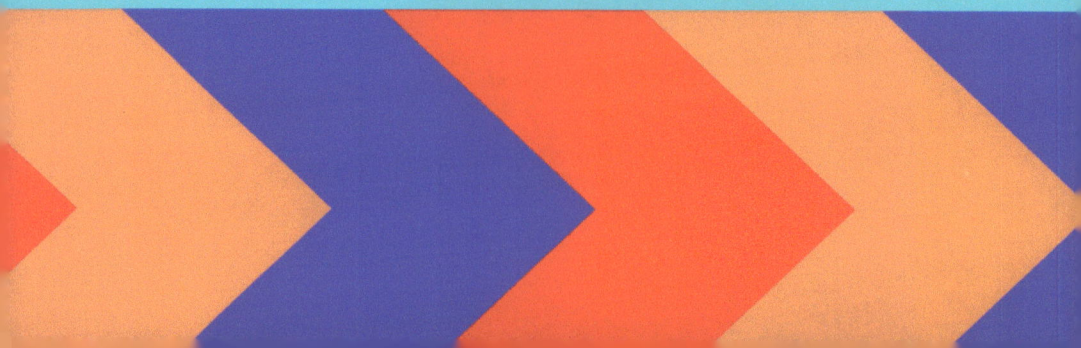

Packaged between two
sympathetic eyes

And a wagging tail full of
promise and hope.

Giving us a living package,

A breathing example
Of His undying love,

He bent low and granted
us an example of His
unyielding love
In the form of a little pup.

Some times I feel so very tired.

So that when our way grew weary,

When our days were
filled with tears,

And our way was hedged
in by uncertainty,

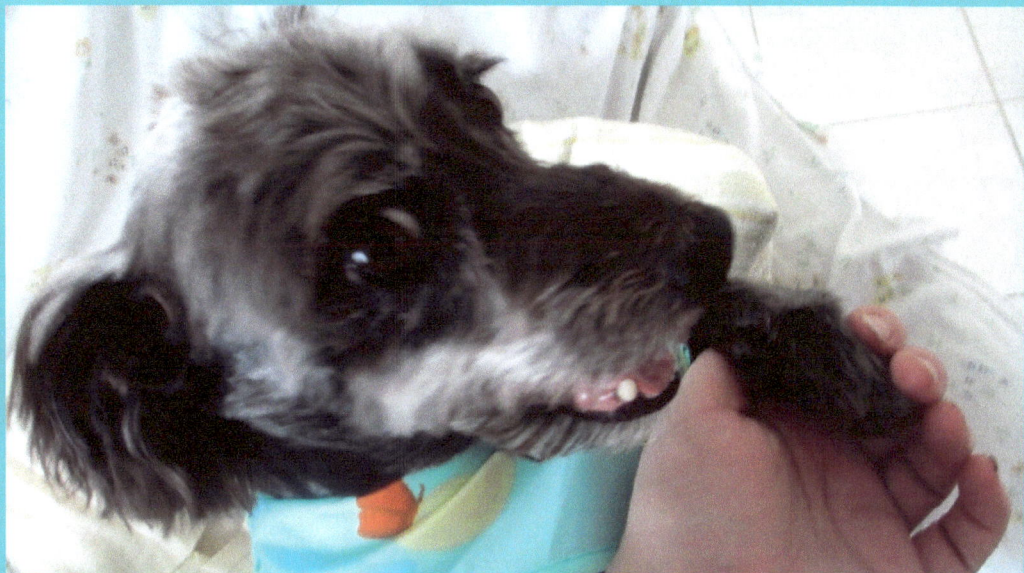

To this precious gift we could turn.

And in spite of our aches
and pains
With glad heart we could
know that through

Our sorrow,
Our tears,

Our joys,

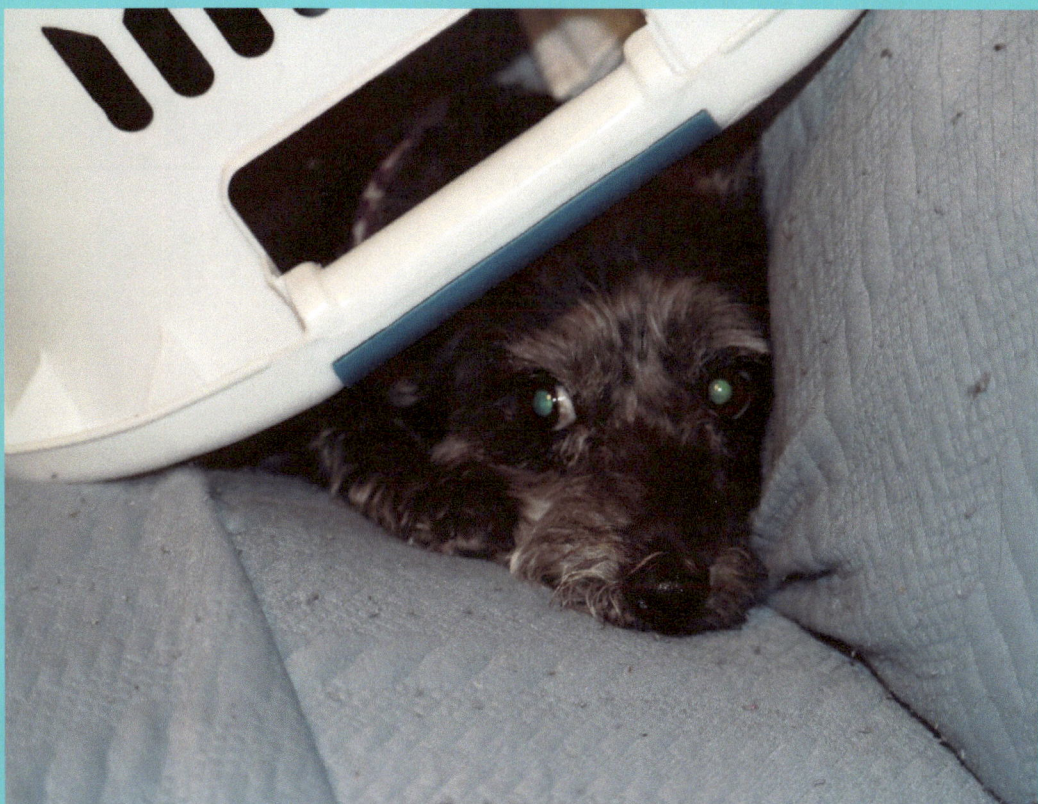

And our fears

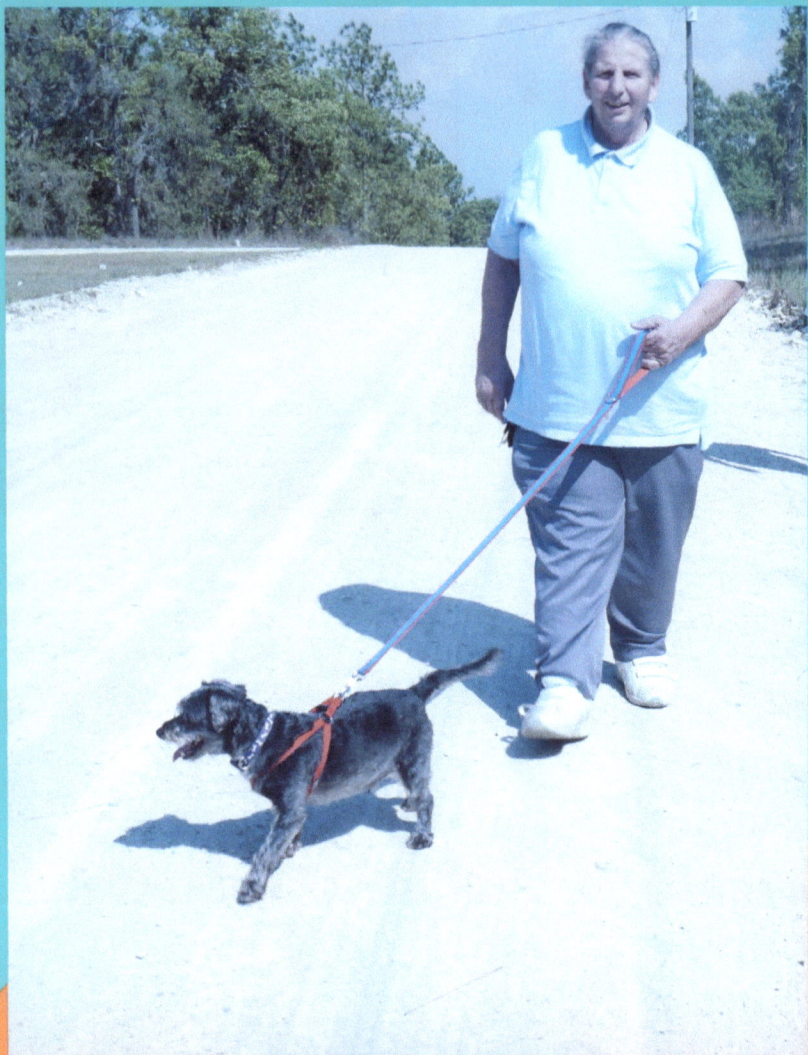

We did not walk the path
of life alone.

www.ingramcontent.com/pod-product-compliance
Lightning Source LLC
Chambersburg PA
CBHW041805040426
42448CB00001B/48